My Song, Our Song

My Song, Our Song

Copyrights
Copyright © 2019 by Iriane McCray

All rights reserved. This book or any portion thereof may not be reproduced or used in any manner whatsoever without the express written permission of the publisher except for the use of brief quotations in a book review or scholarly journal.
First Printing: 2019
ISBN : 978-0-578-21871-7
I'Jale Publishing Co LLC
2431 Manhattan Blvd
Suite C
Harvey, La. 70058
www.ijalepublishing.com

My Song, Our Song

My Song, Our Song

My Song, Our Song

My Song, Our Song

The Intro

My Song, Our Song

Writing has always been my thing. Be it poetry or love letters, I have written outstanding literature for many who have meant the most to me. I've always believed that expressing myself wholeheartedly with words, written or verbal, is the most highest form of honor to give. Acting on this in my adolescence, which wasn't so long ago, introduced me to impulsive behavior and a lack of control. Acting solely on my feelings and making decisions based solely on emotion, I thought that this form of expression would help the person I deemed honorable to recognize my passion and genuity. This mindset led to a combination of many feelings: nothingness and sorrow, anchors of disappointment, and a pain that makes room for a deep wound self-inflicted. I welcomed all of those feelings into my spirit by not honoring myself first.

The realization came that I needed to honor myself when I analyzed the results that I had been getting by choosing to honor others first. Being taken advantage of and taken for granted in my former relationships and friendships sparked the examination of what I was doing wrong. In the past, I had always felt the need to prove myself to those that I love, as if it were a contest to see who loved each other more. I also felt the need to express myself, with hopes of receiving the same honesty in return. But is that truly honest? Why did I feel the need to prove my genuinity by sacrificing my vulnerability? My answer was a bitter truth buried deep: I did not love myself. If I had loved myself, I would not be expectant of receiving a return on the investment of emotional energy I had been giving. Instead I would be giving myself the love that I have expected to receive from others.

Prior to this new realization, I was in the midst of a shift that occurred both internal and external. I moved away from my beloved birthplace, New Orleans, LA, and I embarked on a new chapter in Atlanta,GA for one full year. At first, I viewed this as a pilgrimage to freedom being that I intended to rid myself of all things familiar, besides family and friends, and embark on a new journey with even newer ambitions and adventures. Coming from a way of life that nurtured my happiness was the familiar thing for me. If it didn't bring me happiness or satisfaction, I simply did not do it. At the time I was focused heavily on making my mark as an entrepreneur and educator, and I would frequently encourage people to quit their job or stop doing things that did not give them happiness. The nerve of me! You see, the truth as i have grown to learn it *is that if you are truly happy, then happiness can never leave you; it should be inside you. It doesn't mean that you never get angry or upset, but it means that you know that you know happiness is greater, so you choose it every chance you get. When happiness is inside you, you don't have to search for any accommodations should you feel anything less than bliss.*

You should be present during moments of unhappiness and during rough patches of obstacles that you can't believe are happening to you. Acknowledging this and all the steps that you must take to regain composure and bliss are what make you bulletproof. Nothing can touch you when you know what your intentions are with yourself. You must first acknowledge who you are, and where you are going to really be driven toward accomplishing all goals

My Song, Our Song

and reaching every destination on your journey.

Each of these letters serve as a form of my presence through all situations that i was faced with during this transitional period. Needless to say, I was not joyful or optimistic when I wrote every one of them. At the time I picked up my pen, the only thing that I was in need of was healing, and because I told myself that I am in total control of my own healing from not putting myself first, I committed myself and held myself accountable with these letters.

They started off acting as daily reminders to myself that I am who I think I am, and who God says I am. I needed for my own cup to run over before I could ever try to fill up the cup of another. So many of us who are beautiful people with great intentions want to heal others and help them do the work, when we have yet to do the work ourselves. With that being said, these letters are here for all who have eyes and to help relieve the feeling of loneliness while doing their work. For me, I was interested in other women's stories about their emancipation while I did my work. It wasn't until about a week in doing my rituals of healing that I realized my journey was nothing like the women's whom I appreciated so much, it was entirely different. With that realization came loneliness. I wrote about that too.

These letters are not to serve as a comparison of circumstance, but an aid to acknowledging the power deep within you. Please understand that I am still doing the work, and I will continue because healing myself and others is my heart's joy. Each letter is a song with its own melody and

My Song, Our Song

harmony attached. And like all songs, you can sing together, or alone, loud or soft, with ranging octaves and high notes or with a baritone so beautiful that it will send vibrations throughout the depths of your soul... but my only request is that you pass it on.

My Song, Our Song

Dear You,

I appreciate you seeking out my songs when looking for the soundtrack to your healing. I offer the very heart of me to you, with hopes that every letter written will inspire you to bloom unapologetically; enveloped in acceptance of tainted beauty that is not warranted by perfection. I hope each song tunes the melodies of your soul, and aids in the ease of your journey. Not serving as a road map, but merely a thirst quencher to the traveler. Like your favorite song that gets stuck in your head repeatedly, I hope these letters serve you blissfully.

Love,
Iriane

My Song, Our Song

My Song, Our Song

The Prelude

My Song, Our Song

Dear Self,

Liberate yourself. Tell the truth. Stop harnessing lies with hopes of manifesting a reality. When will you walk proudly in your own truth? For this, you need no permission, only confidence.

Love,
Self

My Song, Our Song

Dear Self,

You are valuable, important, and honest to not only others, but more importantly yourself. You are a profound being who embodies beauty, joy, success, and true wealth. This wealth contains nothing of monetary value, only an abundance of morality. You're not impoverished, you're amazing.

Love,
Self

My Song, Our Song

Dear Self,

You are powerful beyond measure. Anything that comes your way, you deserve. Obstacles are placed in your life to be conquered and missions to be completed. You are destined for greatness and it is your birthright to fulfill your highest destiny. You are the one that you've been waiting for. Make changes to yourself as needed. Make changes to your surroundings as forecasted. Utilize everything that has been revealed to you as evidence; please do not disregard.

Love,
Self

My Song, Our Song

Dear Self,

Always be open to growing stronger! You are on your way to living out your highest destiny. Don't get distracted. Stay the course! At this given moment, you are exactly where you need to be, learning a lesson that is customly created to fit your journey. Get ready to reap one of the greatest harvests yet! Are you prepared?

Love,
Self

My Song, Our Song

Dear Self,

You are beautiful, strong, and intelligent enough to never take any shit off anyone with distorted intentions. The answers are always within you because you are a reflection of the divinity you come from. Behaving in a way that exudes this brings honor to your lineage, anything less is disrespect.

Love,
Self

My Song, Our Song

Dear Self,

Absence and patience work together to develop a fond heart. Refrain from thoughts of discouragement. Don't hesitate to manifest opportunities and make memories that will warm your soul eternally. Smile like the sunshine radiates from your lips and there will be no sign of dusk for about twelve hundred never's.

Love,
Self

My Song, Our Song

Dear Self,

You cannot make anyone love you. If you show persistence in proving your excellence, your worth will depreciate. Always remember that you are special and only special people have absolutely nothing to prove.

Love,
Self

My Song, Our Song

Dear Self,

Even at your lowest smile. Not to pretend or rid of your troubles but smile bright knowing that you have the strength and courage to confront your battles. For every defeat, there is an abundance of victory.

Love,
Self

My Song, Our Song

Dear Self,

Being beautiful is only rewarding when it comes from inside. It is only then that beauty can encompass your entire being and goes beyond the physical. Never be ashamed of your internal beauty in a room full of insecure energy. You are the light intended to ignite their internal flame.

Love,
Self

My Song, Our Song

Dear Self,

Let go of what no longer serves you in confidence. Weak is the person who is afraid to let go. It is physically and mentally demanding to release redundancy. Do not be disappointed. Keep your faith strong and prepare yourself for blessings in abundance.

Love,
Self

My Song, Our Song

Dear Self,

You are the paradigm of what love is. Continue to love yourself wholeheartedly. Continue to be fearless and unapologetic about who you are. Everyone is watching you be you. Leave them all immensely inspired. That is how you truly give thanks for the gifts God has blessed you with.

Love,
Self

My Song, Our Song

Dear Self,

Everything happens for a reason. After it happens, reflect on the reasoning. What caused this to happen? Do what you must to ensure that it either never happens again or continues to happen forever. Be certain of what you want and go for it. Be certain of what you don't want and boldly reject it.

*Love,
Self*

My Song, Our Song

Dear Self,

Love is not painful, nor is it harmful, deceitful, or dishonest. If a loved one potentially displays similar traits, remember it is their willingness to be forgiven and eagerness to show empathy that reveals love in an unappealing form. Love is not always comfortable, but it should always be fulfilling. Never forget, the intense feeling of affection and compassion within the depths of your soul, is designed to be first nurtured by you. After you acknowledge the love that you have for yourself, then acknowledging and recognizing the love that others give you will be easy to see and receive.
    Love,
    Self

My Song, Our Song

Dear Self,

Embrace the power of "No". If you lack the energy to fulfill requests or meet expectations, it is alright to say it unashamed. The power of rejection manifests itself into growth and empowerment. Stop forcing yourself to meet the needs and expectations of others for their singular satisfaction; duality is what you need. Stop feeling defeated once the word is spoken to you Balance is what you must manifest; move forward toward this.

Love,
Self

My Song, Our Song

Dear Self,

Remain patient, holding no regret. Though things may not happen when you want them to, please understand that everything happens in divine time. What is meant for others, may not be meant for you (and likewise). Your journey is uniquely aligned with your blessings. Be ready when they arrive by preparing yourself for the reception of good things.

*Love,
Self*

My Song, Our Song

Dear Self,

Happiness is not forbidden. Love is unstoppable. Indulge in these feelings with yourself proudly. You know that the secret to loving someone on a level that exceeds romanticism, one must love themselves in that same way. It is the one of the safest possible acts to love yourself. For you know that you are the only one accountable for your feelings.

Love,
Self

My Song, Our Song

Dear Self,

Courage is building a vision that can be felt right away but delayed in sight. To manifest these dreams and goals in the physical, continue to visualize them in your life. Act as if you have already received your blessings. Be sure to continuously show extended gratitude for past, present, and future blessings.

*Love,
Self*

My Song, Our Song

Dear Self,

Applaud yourself and Reward yourself. You have come a long way, but you still have a long way to go to achieve success. You have evolved into the kind of person that looks forward to the future because of the excitement it brings. Now embracing the unknown is no longer scary or unfamiliar. Always trust that your steps are ordered by the most high God, who forever guides and protect you every second and every minute.

Love,
Self

Dear Self,

When handling your emotions or the emotions of others, the best approach is maturity. Being fearless in this aspect builds character and illustrates the path of lifelong lessons which can be applied to almost any confrontation. Never should you be afraid of this approach because it is the ultimate release.

Love,
Self

My Song, Our Song

Dear Self,

Your joy is your joy. How you share it is solely up to you. The one thing you must never forget is that your joy belongs to you and comes from you.

Love,
Self

My Song, Our Song

Dear Self,

Think about what you can do to enhance your ability to become more disciplined. Discipline requires mental strength. Refraining from desirable things that are not profitable only decreases the probability of a deterred and delayed journey to victory. Don't condemn the process, welcome it warmly and understand that working for what you want proves your worthiness.

Love,
Self

My Song, Our Song

Dear Self,

Not caring about the feelings of other in order to achieve personal gain comes with consequences that only true savages of the heart can endure. Know yourself and ask yourself if you will humbly accept the consequences. Playing rough with the emotions of others is an action that can be reversed and reciprocated in a way that is unfavorable to you. Don't allow the character flaws of others to disrupt the

Love,
Self

My Song, Our Song

Dear Self,

Don't look back. It is behind you for a reason. Whether it caused you joy or pain, you have conquered that task. It is now time to face the more prevalent obstacles that lie ahead. You can do without luck because you are built to overcome what comes next. It isn't by chance, it is on purpose.

Love,
Self

My Song, Our Song

Dear Self,

Make sure you feel good. This is not a selfish trait. If you do not feel goodness in your heart, denounce the draining energy that is consuming you. Sometimes it is painful to let go of things that have already let go of you. However, the effects from the release hold an immense amount of benevolence. This is when you can feel goodness again.

Love,
Self

My Song, Our Song

Dear Self,

The only person you need is you. Only you can control your circumstance. If something or someone violates your principles and beliefs, it is not your obligation to accept it. The only person you should be fearful of losing in any relationship is yourself.

Love,
Self

My Song, Our Song

Dear Self,

The time that you are focused on him. The time that you sit and await his phone call. The energy spent filtering your thoughts before you speak them to ensure that you are at ease with the response. From the heaviness of doubt, to the uncomfortable portrayal of the woman he wants. It is time to transfer this energy into self-care and self-love. You have earned it. Never neglect your needs to accommodate someone else. Lesson learned.

Love,
Self

My Song, Our Song

Dear Self,

It is not by accident that you are who you are. God designed no one else like you. How you maneuver and navigate through various challenges only enhances your authentic character. Whether or not you realize it, you are second to none when it comes to defeating the odds. Your humility blends so very well with your success. You are more than enough.

*Love,
Self*

My Song, Our Song

Dear Self,

Do not blame or condemn others for not receiving you. The need to be liked only exemplifies insecurity. Those who walk in truth and love do not need recognition or praise from their witnesses. The true praise exists within. The satisfying feeling of bringing joy to someone is most rewarding when it is derived from a pure and genuine heart. Just because others may not wish you well, you're not inadequate. Everything isn't good for everyone, and just anyone isn't good for you.

Love,
Self

My Song, Our Song

Dear Self,

Don't let pride alter your ego. Don't confuse being proud with being prideful. You must never forget the conditions you rose from. Be proud of the ashes. What used to be is what made you who you are now. There is no longer a need to be defensive. Do what you do to fulfill yourself, without criticizing anyone else's process. Growth has no specific instructions.

Love,
Self

My Song, Our Song

Dear Self,

Please be strong against those things that mean you harm. Discipline yourself to reject things based on rationale even if you are caught in the moment. Always be led by your heart, but do not ignore your mind. When you find this balance, you will be unstoppable. Begin when you're ready.

*Love,
Self*

My Song, Our Song

Dear Self,

If someone you have shown only love to, openly rejects you, let them. For it is not you who they are rejecting, it is themselves.

Love,
Self

My Song, Our Song

Dear Self,

Honor your intuition by being obedient; the only intimidating emotion. This is because it requires discipline of the heart and mind. The balance between the rationale of what is and the feeling of what could be will always be a safe space to be obedient. With all decisions your faith should be unwavering. For you will reap the reward, no matter what the outcome is.

Love,
Self

My Song, Our Song

Dear Self,

I need you to disengage from potential for a while. Exist in the now so that you can fully embrace what it is that you really want. It is better to manifest and visualize what you want instead of what you do not. So easily have you been blinded before by possibilities and potential, and now is the time to let go. Try something different... embrace the moments right now, don't overthink them, and take them for what they are.

Love,
Self

My Song, Our Song

Dear Self,

Self- inflicted wounds are the deepest; the longest to heal. Gain back your self-esteem and take control over your life once again. Even the roughest of diamonds shine the brightest under the moonlight.

Love,
Self

My Song, Our Song

Dear Self,

It is okay to have memories. But don't let those memories tempt you into the depths of nostalgia. Just know that each experience with each person had to happen in order to learn and grow. Look at each memory as a positive lesson that you have learned successfully. Prove this by never going back filled with doubt or regret.

Love,
Self

My Song, Our Song

Dear Self,

Always love with courage. Be fearless in love. Do not be timid or shameful. Walk proudly with your head held high that you made the right choice. When the spirit of love chooses you to fall or rise under its' power, you must do so undoubtedly, wholeheartedly, and with great appreciation. Those that are chosen by love will never be forsaken.

*Love,
Self*

Dear Self,

Don't postpone confrontation. Proceed with courage and know that this situation is happening for the sole purpose of improving your life. With a good or bad outcome, the lesson is still valid.

*Love,
Self*

My Song, Our Song

Dear Self,

Impulse can be controlled. Meditate on situations and speak your heart to God. As a result, peace of mind manifests itself so deeply in your life, causing all that worries you to dissipate dramatically. It will hurt, but what comes after feels like the joy the moon feels when it is kissed by the stars.

Love,
Self

My Song, Our Song

Dear Self,

Keep your feet firmly planted on the ground. Understand what you represent, Tranquil is the symbol you wish to embody. Do not overreact to things that will sway you away from your character. Because everything happens for a reason, take everything in stride. With your head held high.

Love,
Self

My Song, Our Song

Dear Self,

Stop searching for what is already inside of you. Acknowledge your greatness. Look within frequently and adhere to the signals and messages of your heart. The most important person to be obedient to is yourself.

*Love,
Self*

My Song, Our Song

Dear Self,

Not loving yourself is self-destruction. To ignore your needs to feed your wants despite immorality and all that you may believe in is painful in hindsight. Alleviate this pain by making good choices. Use the power of discernment to help you navigate through issues that may leave you feeling undecided or pressured.

*Love,
Self*

My Song, Our Song

Dear Self,

You have to accept the consequences of your actions. Do so with the same confidence you had when you did what you did. Don't take any shorts. Be proud. Condemnation comes with guilt. If you are guilty, it is because you did not listen to your heart. Lesson learned.

*Love,
Self*

My Song, Our Song

Dear Self,

Make your future generations proud. Live like they are actively watching everything you do. Love as if you are teaching them the true functions of the heart. Learn your lessons now so that you won't have to learn them together. Take pride in leading by example.

Love,
Self

My Song, Our Song

Dear Self,

Are you running from something? Are you hiding something within yourself? If you are, discover the answers to the questions no matter what. Dig deep and discover the roots; nourish them with the tears you will cry. Remain patient and feel every emotion. Those roots will aid in the development of the beauty that will soon bloom bright and beautiful.

Love,
Self

My Song, Our Song

Dear Self,

Be fearless in everything. There is nothing in this world that can stop you from being aligned with your highest destiny once you acknowledge it. Every obstacle and hurdle was placed here specifically for you to overcome it. Tests of strength and endurance are necessary to be victorious. Even failed attempts have sustainability.

*Love,
Self*

Dear Self,

These are daily words to live by: "Don't stop, Get it Get it!"

*Love,
Self*

My Song, Our Song

Dear Self,

The way to eliminate the things that no longer serve you is not to ignore them. Reject them openly and confidently. Do not become timid. You know exactly what you want and what you don't. This is the first step in receiving what your heart desires.

*Love,
Self*

Dear Self,

In order to be forgiven, you must first forgive others. Release negative energy and feelings. Allow yourself only a short period to feel anger and resentment. Those are natural feelings. But the more minutes you spend dwelling on these emotions, you take away from the hours you can spend dwelling on the bliss and blessings forgiveness brings.

Love,
Self

Dear Self,

Give what you wish to receive. If you wish to receive honesty, you must be honest. You will get what you attract. Everything that you have, remain thankful and proceed to build the life you want to live.

Love,
Self

Dear Self,

Don't depend on anyone to do anything for you, that you can do for yourself. Though you may be a dependable person that others can rely on, do not let this concept influence your relationships and friendships. Understand that everyone is not like you, which is why you are placed in their lives. The sooner you fully understand this, then you will be more comfortable with the outcomes as it relates to others helping you.

Love,
Self

My Song, Our Song

Dear Self,

Refrain from expecting something in return. Sometimes, it is best to be a blessing to those that need you most. Although it is said that you should treat others the way you wish to be treated, do not become overwhelmed with disappointment when someone treats you as if they have damned themselves. Understand that they hurt you because they are hurt themselves. Indulging in your healing will help both of you. Be kind and pay attention.

*Love,
Self*

My Song, Our Song

The Interlude

My Song, Our Song

Dear Self,

You are enough. Enjoy yourself with yourself and bask in your enoughness. Having others around that are unable or unwilling to enjoy you does not make you empty; it makes you lonely. This is the most beautiful and powerful form of loneliness there is; it is from this particular "lack" that love is born.

Love,
Self

Dear Self,

Don't you feel so drained and lethargic when you neglect yourself? Are you holding yourself accountable for this type of neglect? You should be. Prioritizing time for you is valid and critical, not only to your growth, but to your health.

Love,
Self

My Song, Our Song

Dear Self,

Accountability will make everything much more sweeter in your life. Eliminate the sour taste life has right now by holding yourself accountable for the actions you've taken, things you've said and done, and any lack thereof. Your power is strong furthermore enhancing your power of accountability.

*Love,
Self*

My Song, Our Song

Dear Self,

You've ignited the flame burning within you a long time ago. Allow this flame to burn bright, wild, and limitless. If the spark fizzles, remind yourself of what started the fire in the first place. Always hold on to that.

Love,
Self

Dear Self,

Don't forget to prioritize around those things and people that bring you peace. Show them how much they mean to you by staying the course. The real honor comes once the mission has successfully been completed.

Love,
Self

Dear Self,

Do not condemn or celebrate your destination. In reality, you're never really complete with each mission. There will always be another obstacle or hardship. Celebrate the process. Be grateful that you've got the chance at another opportunity. Embrace the joy and the pain that it will bring with control and vigor.

Love,
Self

Dear Self,

Thanks for never giving up. Thanks for always trying your best. Your endurance reflects in your beauty as a person and your ability to remain positive and steadfast no matter the circumstance.

*Love,
Self*

Dear Self,

Preparation is the key. Prepare yourself physically, mentally, and emotionally for everything. Take your time and do the work.

Love,
Self

Dear Self,

Rid of negativity internally and externally. Move on consistently toward positivity and progression. Be fearless in your approach and know that everything that is being removed is giving you space so that you can thoroughly fulfill your highest destiny.

Love,
Self

My Song, Our Song

Dear Self,

Be committed to yourself. Be patient with yourself. You are such a long way from where you started. Be happy! Just know that you aren't anywhere near finished.

Love,
Self

Dear Self,

You are an amazing being and an even more amazing mother. Under no circumstances will you ever be incomplete because you, yourself, are enough.

Love,
Self

My Song, Our Song

Dear Self,

Be joyful on every occasion. Express your joy privately or publicly. Don't be ashamed of your happiness around others who are not experiencing it. Spread joy and always make sure your cup is full!

*Love,
Self*

Dear Self,

Be patient with yourself while you are being patient with others. Trust the process and know that you deserve the same treatment that you give others; this will help you to be mindful of your behavior. However, you must remember that you can't treat anyone better than you treat yourself. That is an unnecessary pain.

Love,
Self

My Song, Our Song

Dear Self,

Manage your time properly. Don't become overwhelmed and start underappreciating the process. The process consists of long nights, hard times, and consistent care for yourself. Do not be delayed.

Love,
Self

My Song, Our Song

Dear Self,

Continue to be kind, show gratitude continuously, as well, despite what others are doing or have done to you. Remember those negative experiences have turned positive because there was a lesson learned. Nothing and no one can harm you without your consent. Emotions are all about perception, and you have the power to perceive positivity in all things.

Love,
Self

My Song, Our Song

Dear Self,

Do not compromise yourself for anyone. Someone who loves you will not ask you to compromise self. They will meet you where you are and love you beyond all limits aiding in your quest to reach your fullest potential.

*Love,
Self*

My Song, Our Song

Dear Self,

Have an amazing day! Remember that your altitude is determined by your attitude. Remember to be mindful of all circumstances you're currently enduring, and all situations that you are placed in. Take your time reflecting, and don't let anything overwhelm you.

       Love,
       Self

My Song, Our Song

Dear Self,

Discipline and Sacrifice are the same. The melody and the tempo may differ, but the song is the same. Sing proudly and loudly for all to hear. Everyone is watching. Ancestors are watching. It is your duty to make them proud to have you uphold the legacy of strength, courage, and victory.

Love,
Self

My Song, Our Song

Dear Self,

Be consistent with yourself, even if others are not. It doesn't matter if someone who's important to you did not fulfill your wishes or honor your request. Find a way or ways to get it done! You won't have a consistency of let downs, if you are consistent about keeping yourself up. Allow you to become your main focus. Appreciate the process, and more importantly…appreciate yourself.

Love,
Self

My Song, Our Song

Dear Self,

Allow appreciation, gratitude, (or whatever you choose to identify this feeling as) to fill up your heart and soul. Everything that you believed, you are seeing! Everything you have dreamt, you are now living! Everything that you have, has been manifested by You! Continue to do the work being the master and creator of all of what you seek. Know that your growth is phenomenal and will be endless.

Love,
Self

My Song, Our Song

Dear Self,

Know your value. Do not become disappointed in yourself if you entertain things that depreciate your value. Understand that these experiences are for learning purposes only, and your quest is knowledge of self. Recharge and execute, everything will be just fine.

Love,
Self

My Song, Our Song

Dear Self,

The journey you have traveled thus far has been long, but there is much more to go. You are preparing yourself well, but don't forget to celebrate your wins and losses equally because of their purpose. Victory and defeat have worked together cohesively to help shape you into the bulletproof being that you are. Nothing can touch you and no one can stop you.

Love,
Self

My Song, Our Song

Dear Self,

Healing yourself has become your heart's joy. Don't be so critical of others who haven't experienced this joy just yet. Just like you, they are on their own journey. You are the example or the proof that they need in order to continue this part of their journey. For some, sometimes seeing is believing. Allow all changes that you're experiencing to be a vessel in helping others heal. Understand that you are chosen to do this work. Give thanks.

Love,
Self

My Song, Our Song

Dear Self,

Handle things with ease. There is no need to get riled up. Understand that you are in control over what things deserve your energy. Know that you are valuable and not everything needs or deserves a reaction from you. Especially circumstances that are not deeply rooted in peace.
Love,
  Self

My Song, Our Song

Dear Self,

Understand that loving someone else is not as easy as it looks. Love is work. Those that are willing to put in the work, commit to sacrifices, and are open to evolving, will flourish in love. Those that are focused on patience and have removed their ego are growing in love. And those that ignore the work become stuck or stagnant in love because they felt too deep without any armor to shield them from love's trials. What are you doing in love? Have you full accepted this commitment? Are you ready to do the work? Just know that you are equipped to withstand hardships and heartaches, highs and lows, because of the love you have for yourself, and that love is the most healing.

Love,

Self

My Song, Our Song

Dear Self,

You owe it to yourself to execute all tasks and goals that you set. Now is your time to shine! Forget about fear and understand the components of failure, those elements are non-existent in your plan and will not stop you from reaching and living out your highest destiny. Get it done! This time, and every time. Everything that you have always wanted is yours...all you must do is maintain the rhythm and speed up the tempo, claim it all and prepare to feel feelings you have never felt before.

Love,
Self

My Song, Our Song

The Outro

My Song, Our Song

Each of these letters has reminded me that I have made the right decision in choosing myself first. However, I cannot take full credit for the motivation and inspiration behind sharing all of what I have felt over the years. To be totally transparent has always been my goal, but if it were not for my amazing support system then I would not have had enough courage to do so. It is because of you, that I am.

Mo dupe O Olodumare! I give thanks to God! The most high God of all things! The God of balance, divinity, honesty, and prosperity. I am everything you are. I am equipped with the power that is within me and has been since the day that I was born. It is my birthright to experience joy and happiness. It is the closeness to you that reveals my true and highest self. It is my *love for God that has allowed me to show love and experience love with myself. It is God who accompanied me on those lonely days and nights when I felt inadequate and undeserving. It is God who has healed me from the inside out, allowing me to see who I am. It is God who understands me, when I don't even understand myself. I am eternally grateful for the peace and unwavering strength and endurance that is within me, for I know that I am only created in your beautiful and majestic image.*

Nia, the most wonderful daughter and the most amazing person I've ever known. You are love. You are the personification of benevolence and bliss. I love you beyond the concept of any beautifully written word or phrase. I love you beyond space and time. It is because of you, that I have evolved into the woman that I know now. It is your

My Song, Our Song

presence alone that helped me seek and find my purpose. Never forget your power, but should you for whatever reason, I hope these letters find you well. Your journey is yours, and I am so grateful that I was chosen to be a part of it.

To my parents, my Mothers and Father. You each have played an instrumental part in my healing. I thank God every day for the love that you have surrounded me with each and every day of my life. You have instilled in me the fundamental concept that "with God, nothing is impossible". Though I have strayed away from believing, and most of the time, listening, I have never stopped learning from you. Being my teacher could not have been easy, I thank you for embracing me in my stubborn moments and encouraging me during my lowest points. I cannot even begin to give you the amount

My Song, Our Song

of thanks you deserve; I love you is an understatement.

To my love, I will love you forever. You inspire me to be a better version of myself. Even though I only keep you around so that you will laugh at all my jokes, I thank you for everything.

To my friends, thank you for always seeing my potential. Thank you for being amazing and listening to me when I needed your ears most. Thanks for answering the phone no matter what time it is. Thanks for smiling with me, crying with me, laughing with me, and learning with me. Our journey together is far from over. We are forever, like journals and pens.

My Song, Our Song

To my siblings, I love all six of you. We have something that others smile upon. I am grateful for our love and the support that you give me consistently, no matter if I'm right or wrong. You give my heartbeat a unique rhythm...my tribe.

My Song, Our Song

www.ingramcontent.com/pod-product-compliance
Lightning Source LLC
Chambersburg PA
CBHW032058150426
43194CB00006B/570